EMBRACING
FORGIVENESS

Nothing in your life is beyond God's ability to do something about it.

Forgiveness takes more strength than you have. It takes His.

Forgiveness is in many ways a gift to ourselves.

EMBRACING FORGIVENESS

Foreword by Nicole Johnson

THOMAS NELSON
Since 1798

NASHVILLE   DALLAS   MEXICO CITY   RIO DE JANEIRO   BEIJING

The publishers are greatful to Katharine E. Harris for her collaboration and writing skills in developing the content of this study guide.

Published in Nashville, Tennessee, by Thomas Nelson. Thomas Nelson is a registered trademark of Thomas Nelson, Inc.

Thomas Nelson, Inc. titles may be purchased in bulk for educational, business, fund-raising, or sales promotional use. For information, please e-mail SpecialMarkets@ThomasNelson.com.

ISBN 978-1-4185-2939-0

Printed in China

08 09 10 11 12 MT 5 4 3 2 1

Contents

Foreword   vii

Introduction   ix

Understanding the Need for Forgiveness   xi

1   God Is Light   1

2   Stepping into the Light   7

3   God Is Just   15

4   Being Sorry for Sin: Understanding Repentance   23

Crying Out for Forgiveness: God Offers Hope   31

5   God Is Merciful   33

6   Forgive Me!   41

7   God Seeks Sinners   49

8   For a Worthless Sinner?   57

Embracing the Power of Forgiveness   65

9   God's Forgiveness Is Complete: He Brings Restoration   67

10 Embracing Forgiveness   75

Contents

11 The Clean Slate   81

12 Forgive As You Have Been Forgiven   89

Leader's Guide   97

Foreword

Embracing Forgiveness: Does God Really Forgive me?

"You have to forgive yourself." I've heard those words more times than I can count. And I'm guessing you have too.

Usually when we wonder out loud, "Does God really forgive me?" someone reassures us with an emphatic, "Yes, He does." Then they might add something like, "But you have to forgive yourself too."

I've thought quite a bit about this. Perhaps it is because I have struggled deeply to understand how God's generous and gracious offer of forgiveness can be real. Many of us who believe in God are asking, "Does God really forgive me?" but in a different way: "If God forgives me, then why don't I feel forgiven?"

It is hard to believe that God really does forgive us. It's almost too good to be true, so we disbelieve it and move on to what we think to be the deeper challenge of forgiving ourselves. But we can't forgive ourselves. We don't have it in us; forgiveness is too big and too hard.

That's why God sent Christ to redeem the world, so we could find real forgiveness for ourselves in Him. This is what it means to have a Savior.

Can a person who has molested a child decide he should just forgive himself for what he has done? Can a thief simply say, "I've forgiven myself for stealing from others"? A spouse who has deceived the other cannot say, "Well, I've forgiven myself; why can't you just move on?" There are consequences when we wrong others that no amount of positive thinking can erase.

If the wages of sin is death, how can we absolve ourselves? Whose rules did you break? Whose trust did you violate? What does granting our own forgiveness have to do with anything? Forgiveness must be granted by the one who was wronged in order to have true reconciliation.

Thinking we can forgive ourselves might actually be an affront to God. If we could simply forgive ourselves, then Christ's sacrifice was a waste of time. But as we delve into this study, we will gain a deeper understanding of what it means to be forgiven by God and how that understanding can help dissolve our guilt and help us feel truly forgiven.

Forgiveness must cost something. If forgiveness is free, it is cheap and worthless. Too many people think God's forgiveness is so free that they can spread it around like salt on the open wounds of the wronged in this world. While God's forgiveness is freely available to us, it was not free; the cost was enormous.

Our work in answering the question of this study is to focus on what it takes to understand and accept God's forgiveness in the deepest parts of our souls. We begin with an intellectual understanding of what He did to secure our forgiveness, and that knowing works its way from our heads to our hearts, little by little, all the way down to the tips of our fingers and toes. Knowing we are forgiven causes tears to flow and laughter to break out and gratitude to rise up inside our whole being.

My prayer, when you close this study, is that you will have the ability and the assurance to answer "Does God really forgive me?" with a resounding and reverberating, "Yes!"

—Nicole Johnson

Introduction

We've all seen children squabbling with each other. In fact, we've all been those squabbling children. One child says something that hurts the other's feelings, maybe one smacks the other. Whatever happens, we all know the bad feeling that quarreling gives. In fact, after a quarrel, a group of children can be grumpy for the rest of the day. It's the same when we're grown up. When we act badly, we feel badly. When people mistreat us, we hurt, and sometimes we hurt them back. We all know the feeling of being "out of whack" with our world, and the need to be put right.

Anyone who spends time with children has seen the power of a simple, "I'm sorry," followed by a simple, "I forgive you," to restore harmony. It feels like the badness can then be forgotten, and friendship can go on.

The remedy is the same for us as adults, but somehow we have a much harder time putting it into practice than children do. We all know about forgiveness, but we don't always know how to embrace it into our own lives. Sometimes this is because we don't realize that we need forgiveness. We may vaguely wonder why we feel mixed up and unhappy, but we are pretty self-satisfied, and don't believe that we might be at fault. Sometimes it is because we are so bruised and burdened by our own sins that we don't know how to let them go. Our "forgetters" don't work very well, and we continue to carry baggage that we need to throw away. We think it is tied to us forever, and are hopeless for relief.

The truth is that God offers hope for our burdened state. He has made a way for us to be cleansed and forgiven. He is ready and waiting to take us back, and to lead us into abundant life.

To begin understanding the power of forgiveness, we need to understand something about who God is, and also about who we really are. When we see God's holiness contrasted with our darkness, we begin to understand our need. Learning what God's requirements are shows us where we fall short. Understanding God's just character as a positive attribute gives us hope that He will make all things right, while at the same time showing how serious sin can be.

When we realize our deep need for forgiveness, we must also be reassured of God's mercy and love. God is not only able to forgive sinners, He actively seeks sinners to bring back into His family. God's forgiveness is available, but He wants us to desire it and to tell Him of that desire.

Understanding and embracing God's forgiveness is absolutely essential to living a victorious and purposeful life. God's forgiveness is no halfway measure: He not only forgives; He restores and renews our lives. He rebuilds what we have torn down. He fills in all our holes. The apostle Paul said it best: *"He has delivered us from the power of darkness and conveyed us into the kingdom of the Son of His love, in whom we have redemption through His blood, the forgiveness of sin"* (Colossians 1:13–14).

May the Lord bless you as you seek and find the cleansing, restoring power of His forgiveness.

Understanding the Need for Forgiveness

Before we can receive forgiveness, we must learn that we need forgiveness. We need to learn not only who God is, but also who we really are. Probably none of us are brash enough to think we're perfect, but how clearly do we see ourselves?

One

God Is Light

The people who walked in darkness have seen a great light;
Those who dwelt in the land of the shadow of death,
Upon them a light has shined.

ISAIAH 9:2

Did you know that statistically speaking, people who live in areas with little sunshine are more prone to depression? It is true. The parts of the world that are very dark in winter have a much higher rate of clinical depression than brighter locales. Now obviously there is more to depression than the number of hours of daylight we enjoy, but most people would agree that light and darkness do affect our moods. We associate sunlight with energy, cheerfulness, and purpose, while grey days often make us feel dull, quiet, and sedentary.

Many times in His Word, God uses an illustration that we understand very well: the contrast between light and darkness. This "light versus dark" illustration speaks strongly to us because we rely so heavily on our sight to help us get around. We also know how sudden bright light hurts our unaccustomed eyes.

Not too long ago, I accidentally locked myself out of the house, and had to "break in" through the basement. It was dark, and the light switch is inconveniently located at the top of the stairs. Now, I know my basement pretty well, and it isn't all that big. Nevertheless, in creeping across it in the dark, I managed to bump into just about everything possible. Even when you think you know where you are going, stumbling around in the dark is a good way to bang your elbows and stub your toes.

Can you imagine how absurd it would have been if I had had a light, but had refused to turn it on because I didn't want to see how messy my basement was? I found out exactly how messy it was by tripping over the things on the floor. Yes, the light would have shown the mess, but it also would have saved my skin.

We often stumble around in our lives in just the same way, tripping over the furniture, and sometimes each other. And we are so accustomed to it, that we don't want to change. We think we like the dark, and we are scared of what the light might show. Sure, we know there's a mess (don't we trip over it all the time?), but somehow not "seeing" it makes us willing to go on being hurt by it.

But God has a better plan for us. We may be used to the bruises we get from banging around in the dark, thinking it's "normal," but that's not the way God means for us to live. God desires for us to live abundant lives, filled with light and love. He wants us to experience the cleansing power of forgiveness; to be able to see where we are going so that we can move forward with purpose and confidence. And He wants us to not only walk in the light, but to be filled with light.

1. Read 1 John 1:5–7. This passage tells us that God is light. What is darkness?

2. Why is someone who walks in darkness not able to be in fellowship with God?

God could have left us to stumble around by ourselves, but instead, He has planned an opportunity for us to choose the light.

3. Read **John 3:16–21**. Who or what is "the world"? How could God's Son save the world?

4. Who is condemned? Why?

> *God desires for us to live abundant lives, filled with light and love.*

5. What is the light that has come into the world? Read **John 1:1–13** as you think about this question.

6. What does it mean to "come into the light"? How can you do this?

A large, busy family had reached out to a number of troubled young people, offering the warmth of their home to kids who were missing the nurturing they needed. Sometimes this turned out better than others, but one young man was particularly difficult. He obviously liked them, but wherever he was, there seemed to be constant turmoil. One day, he unwittingly gave them the clue to his problem as he commented, "I just don't feel like I'm really living unless there is some conflict going on." The turmoil he lived in was of his own making; not so much because he loved it but because he was used to it. A high level of emotional upheaval and discomfort was his "normal," but to most of us, "normal" is what feels safe.

7. *Why might someone prefer darkness? Have you ever been in a situation where you wanted to choose darkness over light? What happened?*

8. *Read* **Ephesians 5:8–14.** *Who are the children of light? How does a child of light walk?*

Digging Deeper

The apostle John wrote a great deal about God as light; the last chapter of the book of Revelation continues this theme. Read **Revelation 22:1–5**. How does this picture of the heavenly city fit in with what we have been discussing? Who will enjoy this place with God?

Ponder and Pray

Read **Psalm 119:105**. In what way does God's Word function as a lamp? What can you do to make better use of this light?

Bonus Activity

Every morning we are given a graphic picture of light overcoming darkness. Make an effort this week to watch at least one sunrise, and thank God for the Light that came into the world.

Two

Stepping into the Light

For all have sinned and fall short
of the glory of God.

ROMANS 3:23

Recently, several authors have been writing about the problems that Mean Girls cause for other girls. While popular thought often portrays bullying as physical violence, we all know that "sticks and stones may break bones, *but words cause damage too!*"

Most of us have probably known a Mean Girl or two in our lives, from school or work or our childhood neighborhoods. Do you remember what she did or said that made her a Mean Girl to you? Do you think she remembers it that way?

Chances are good that she doesn't, because no one likes to think of *herself* as "That Mean Girl."

I still remember the Mean Girl in my class. It began during a rainy first-grade recess when we were all sitting on the steps drawing with our new markers. Up until this time, the rest of the children in my class had not sorted themselves out of a nameless blur of strangers, but after this day, one girl stood out forever: Miranda, That Mean Girl.

It was quite simple in the beginning. Miranda, looking for something to spice things up a bit, turned to my trusting friend Emma. "Hey Emma," she said, "Write your name in marker on the steps."

"Okay," Emma said obligingly. I gasped. Our teacher had given us permission to take our markers to recess, with the strict injunction to only write on our papers.

"No, Emma! Don't!" I cried. But I was too late. A sprawling purple E M M A decorated the second step. Intoxicated with the novelty, Emma quickly wrote her name two more times. Horrified, I picked up my black marker, and firmly (and self-righteously) crossed out Emma's writing. Miranda watched the whole proceeding with interest, and then—treachery of all treachery!—she ran out and called the playground supervisor.

It was an awful afternoon. The playground supervisor was a fierce, tall woman, who turned us over without mercy to the terrible janitor. I was quaking in my pink Velcro tennis shoes, but Emma, who apparently was made of sterner stuff, looked nonchalant. The terrible janitor scolded us vigorously and even Emma's *sang-froid* deserted her. We both burst into tears and spent the rest of the afternoon sitting on our teacher's lap and howling. The unbelievable crowning treachery was when Miranda unblushingly denied all knowledge of the whole affair. I was so ashamed to tell my mother that I had been in trouble at school. I was a Good Girl; I wasn't the sort who made trouble. It was all that Mean Girl's fault.

It wasn't until a few years later that I learned a different viewpoint to the story. I was in a different school by then, and idly remembering that dreary wet day in first grade. *Miranda sure was mean,* I thought. *I wonder what she's like now. Nasty, I bet.* Then came a thought, blinding in its novelty. *Clarice probably remembers you as "That Mean Girl." But you don't think of yourself that way, do you? You think of yourself as a nice girl.*

I thought that Miranda was mean, but I had been much, much

worse. I was having a birthday party, and because we had invited only four children to come, my mother gave me strict instructions not to talk about my birthday at school. It would be rude to let everyone know I was having a party and not invite them all. I cheerfully agreed, and feeling on top of the world, had a very enjoyable day. After school, my friend Rachel and I were hanging around the schoolyard waiting for my big sister when I saw Clarice, the not so clean, "difficult" child in our class. As I, the "nice child," waited for my nice big sister to walk me home to our nice house where my mother was cooking a nice supper for us, I turned to Clarice and said, "I'm having a birthday party, and you are NOT invited. Rachel is coming, but not you." Clarice didn't say anything. She just stood there.

We flounced off together, but I didn't quite want to look at Rachel. I felt guilty and almost puzzled. There was no reason to be mean to Clarice. I had had a good day. I was generally obedient to Mama's instructions, even if she wasn't there. I had just opened my mouth and let it spill out. I knew I would be punished if my mother knew; my father and sister would be shocked at my nastiness. I knew that Rachel didn't feel good about me either, even though she'd joined me. But I still didn't believe I was a Mean Girl. I quickly pushed the whole incident to the back of my mind.

Even if we forget our own sins, God does not. When He brought it to my mind again, I was so ashamed! I didn't know Clarice anymore, and couldn't even say, "I'm sorry." I knew she would always remember *me* as "That Mean Girl," just as I remembered Miranda that way.

I found out that even a Nice Girl can be That Mean Girl, because our badness comes from inside. No one else made me act badly. That was the stinky part of the Real Me.

Human sinfulness isn't something any of us are eager to claim as our birthright. Sure, we know we're not perfect, but we view our shortcomings with a pretty indulgent eye. We tell ourselves that it either "wasn't that bad" or it "wasn't my fault." This seems comfortable, but in fact it is destructive. We can't be free until we are willing to step into the light and see our sins for what they are. Stepping into God's light is the first step to forgiveness and cleansing.

1. *How would you describe yourself as a child (think of one or two words)? How do you think your childhood friends remember you? What about your parents?*

In C. S. Lewis's book *The Silver Chair,* the girl Jill is given a quest to find the lost Prince of Narnia. To guide her on her way, Aslan gives her four "signs," which she must memorize. Every one of the signs is literally fulfilled, but every one looks quite different from her expectations. Jill nearly misses the way more than once because she becomes preoccupied with her own problems, and relies on how she thinks the sign may be fulfilled rather than on what Aslan actually told her. Do we actually know what God expects of us, or are we relying on our own ideas of goodness?

2. The Ten Commandments are often thought of as "the basics" of being a "good person." Let's take a closer look. Read **Exodus 20:1–17**. How many of these commands do you think you could recite without looking? How well do you think you have kept them?

3. In simple language, what does God require of us? (Read **Luke 10:27** and **Micah 6:8**). Give practical examples.

4. Read *Matthew 5:19–22; 27–30; 43–48*. What is Jesus getting at in this sermon?

5. Are sins of action worse than or different from sins of the heart? Do they have different consequences?

6. What insight does this sermon give you into how you keep God's commands?

7. Read **Luke 5:27–32**. What kind of people is Jesus interested in calling to follow Him? Why would He choose these people?

8. Is there anyone who does not need Jesus? Who are the righteous?

> **We can't be free until we are willing to step into the light and see our sins for what they are.**

9. What qualifies a person as a sinner? What is sin?

Digging Deeper

Why do we need to remember our sins? Why can't we just forget them and go on to better things?

Ponder and Pray

Looking at sin isn't very comfortable, but it is necessary. Admission is the first step to the freedom and cleansing of forgiveness. Read **Psalm 139** (particularly the last two verses). Can you join the psalmist in this prayer? What does this psalm say to you about how well God already knows you?

Bonus Activity

Try to read **Psalm 19:14** every day this week. Write it down and place it somewhere where you will see it every day.

Three

God Is Just

And there is no other God besides Me,
A just God and a Savior;
There is none besides Me.

ISAIAH 45:21

Acknowledging sin is hard; sometimes simply because it is ugly, sometimes because we fear punishment. No one finds it easy to see herself as bad person. The temptation is to either excuse our behavior or to deny it. But we all know that God is fully aware of all the secrets that we fondly imagine are hidden from sight. The question is not how to keep Him from finding out; the question is what He is going to do about it.

What are your preconceived ideas of God? Do you see Him as a harsh, judgmental dictator, waiting for you to trip up so He can blast you? Or perhaps you see Him as a kindly grandfather, helping you up and saying, "Don't worry, honey, I just love you." It is interesting that such erroneous views of God are actually two sides of the same misconception of God's justice. We often view the just character of God as something negative, and would rather focus on His love. But the fact is that God could not be loving if He were not also just.

Justice is a very important concept to us. I believe that humans are hardwired to desire and recognize justice just as we are wired to desire and recognize freedom. We're not very good at finding it, but the need is always there. Think about the squabbles of little children, and how often they are centered on some injustice, perceived or real. The favorite cry of children is "It's not fair!" or "She did such and such first!" When something wrong happens, we want it fixed. We don't want it overlooked or ignored. We want justice! Of course the problem is that this cuts both ways. We aren't always so eager for justice when we are the sinners. That is when we would rather have mercy.

Have you ever seen the traditional statues or pictures of Justice personified? Justice is always shown as a woman, blindfolded, with a balance scale in her hand. The idea is to show that true justice is no respecter of persons. Justice can't be bribed or influenced, but always weighs the truth on her scales honestly. Justice gives what is coming to you, no more and no less. In many ways, there is a real feeling of security in knowing that justice will be served. If you have been badly treated, you want to know that the perpetrator has been dealt with, or that you have been reimbursed. Even when you are the one who has sinned, there is a certain relief in making restitution, setting right what you made wrong. The problem is, there are some sins that we can never set right. The damage we have done is far beyond our ability to repair, and even beyond this, our relationship with God is broken. The world cries out for justice, but at the same time, justice is more than we can bear.

The lovely truth is that God, unlike anyone else, is both just and a savior. He does not overlook sin, or say, "It doesn't matter, honey." Just think how awful it would be to think that God didn't notice or care when terrible things happen to you! Or how wrong it would be if God didn't care about the hurts you inflicted on other people, just because He didn't want you to "feel bad." No, in order for God to be God, He has to be concerned with justice. But God doesn't have to be blind-folded in order to weigh justly. It is true that Justice is no respecter of persons, and neither is God. You won't get off the hook by being extra cute, or rich, or smart, or even by being a victim. Sin is sin. God is not only just, He is a savior. That means that He makes a way for sinners, like you and me, to be rescued from the consequences of our sins—not just be "let off the hook."

1. Read **Romans 3:20–26**. *This passage uses a lot of big words, but they are good words with very specific meanings. Take a moment or two to talk about the meanings of these important words.*

   justified: declared righteous. This word is also an accounting term—an account that is "justified" is one that balances, one where everything adds up.

   propitiation: atonement, the act of satisfying God's wrath against sin, the act of paying for or conciliating. Jesus' blood, as propitiation, was payment for our sins.

2. Read **Romans 3:23** again, and also **Romans 6:23**. According to these verses, what would happen to us if we received impartial justice?

3. What is "the redemption that is in Christ Jesus" (Rom. 3:24)?

4. How does this redemption demonstrate God's righteousness?

We are all very familiar with the trying to justify ourselves. It has been said that "anger is the great justifier." When you are angry, don't you just *feel* that you are right? The problem is that we don't have the right or the power to justify ourselves. In fact, self-justification is also known as "making excuses." Sure, it's easy to "declare yourself righteous" to the police officer who has pulled you over for a traffic violation. But do you think that is going to keep you from getting a ticket? Of course not! The officer is not interested in whether you think you were justified, he is concerned with the fact that you broke the law.

5. *Who has the right to justify? Why?*

6. *What does it mean for God to be both just and a justifier?*

7. *Read* **1 John 1:9.** *John describes God's faithfulness and justice as resulting in two things: forgiveness and cleansing. Why is it important that these two things go together?*

> *God is not only just, He is a savior. That means that He makes a way for sinners, like you and me, to be rescued from the consequences of our sins—not just be "let off the hook."*

8. *Since God already knows all about us, why is confession important? Why doesn't God just forgive us right off?*

9. *How specific do you think you should be in confession? Why?*

Digging Deeper

We have talked about the results of impartial justice. What are the results of justification? Read **Romans 5:1–2.**

Ponder and Pray

In our time of "ultra-tolerance," God's justice is often portrayed as harsh and "judgmental." In the human sense, the negative connotations of the word *judgmental* are probably justified because we are so often wrong in our judgments—we're both hard-hearted and soft-headed. But in reference to God, He is the only one with the right to judge, and we need Him to do it.

Ironically, God is also bitterly criticized for not judging those who bring about terrible wickedness, like genocide and war and hatred. Rest assured, God is not ignorant of the wickedness of this world. God cares deeply for justice. Read **Psalm 82:1–4.** In what situation do you cry out for justice? Talk to God about this, and thank Him for His justice and also for His mercy.

Bonus Activity

Write out **Isaiah 45:21** on an index card or sticky note and stick it to your bathroom scales. When you weigh in, read it to remind yourself that God not only weighs justly, He also made a way to save you!

Four

Being Sorry for Sin: Understanding Repentance

For I acknowledge my transgressions,
And my sin is always before me.
Against You, You only, have I sinned,
And done this evil in Your sight.

PSALM 51:3–4

In studying different cultures around the world, anthropologists are always interested in trying to figure out what makes people "tick." Why do certain things seem to be acceptable in one culture, but are considered bad or weird in others? Most importantly, what defines a culture's sense of morality? These subjects become especially interesting when two cultures merge, for instance when a non-Western nation sets up a Western-style democracy; or when a tribal culture moves to the big cities and becomes part of a modern urban setting.

One of the things that has been discovered is how the various cultures view transgressions. Every culture has certain things that they consider unacceptable. But exactly how people deal with a failure to keep the code can be quite varied.

There are two primary categories—shame-oriented societies and guilt-oriented societies. In a shame-oriented society, the shame of being caught is the strongest deterrent from sin. This system is quite effective in a tribal/village culture or a close, extended family where people are accustomed to being in close contact with one another. They know all about every detail of each other's lives. It is hard to "break the rules" without someone finding out. This doesn't work so well in a setting with more privacy, where the bad things can be done behind closed doors, and modern conveniences of transportation and communication make it easy to cover your tracks. If no one finds out, there is no aspect of public shame to your transgression. Essentially, if you can get away with it, you're free.

A guilt-oriented society, on the other hand, relies on a person's inner sense of right and wrong (programmed by the culture) to keep him or her from going over the line. In this kind of society, a person is expected to feel personally guilty of sin, whether or not anyone finds out. Guilt is usually associated with some level of belief that God is watching us, and knows our secrets.

Thinking about the difference between guilt and shame can give us some insight into how we deal with our own sins, and specifically how we handle repentance.

Guilt is a more interior reaction, based on what we think of ourselves and what God thinks of us. We can feel guilty about something that no one else knows about, or maybe even something that others don't consider wrong. Guilt is conscience-based rather than reputation-based.

Shame essentially comes from the outside—it is based on fear of what others will think of us when they know how bad we are. While shame pushes us to hide, guilt pushes us to try to repair. And when guilt and shame mix, it is very hard to bear.

When we do wrong things, usually one of two things happens: we get caught, or what we did brings bad consequences. It is easy to be sorry that you got caught in the act; it's so embarrassing and humiliating to be obviously and inexcusably wrong. It is also easy to be sorry for the bad consequences of our sins. It is impossible to dish out sin without getting something back for it. Sin has a way of acting like a boomerang. We toss it off without a care, and then when we aren't looking it comes back and gets us in the neck.

Real repentance is more than saying, "I'm sorry I got caught," or "I'm sorry I tasted the fruit because I didn't like the flavor." These kinds of "sorry" are certainly real emotions, but they never deal with the heart of the problem. They never deal with the fact that every sin is really a sin against God.

Yes, sin will hurt you personally. When you sin, you will undoubtedly wound others as well. But most serious of all is the fact that your sin will be a barrier between you and God. And without God's help, we don't have a hope of living in freedom and light.

1. Read 2 Corinthians 7:8–11. Does sorrow necessarily lead to repentance? Where else might it lead?

2. What is godly sorrow? What is the sorrow of the world?

3. It appears that being sorry and repenting are not the same. What is repentance? Does repentance include sorrow?

4. Read **Luke 19:1–10.** Was Zacchaeus sorry for his sins? Did he repent? What tells you this?

Shame has great power. In a shame-oriented society, as we have seen, this power is partially used for good in that it is used to prevent people from sinning. However, the power of shame also has a very negative side, because it is a power of inaction rather than action. Shame may prevent you from committing sin, but it is also very powerful in preventing you from being released from sin. Shame naturally makes us want to hide our sins—and it is true, we should be ashamed, if what we have done is wrong! But as long as we hide our sins, we cannot be forgiven. Remember what we read last week? Confession, forgiveness, cleansing. It goes in that order.

5. Read **James 5:16**. *Does this idea scare you? What might be the dangers of confessing "to one another"?*

6. *Who should the "one another" be? Why? Are there people to whom you should not confess your sins?*

7. What is the power in confessing "to one another"? How should you respond if someone confesses something to you?

> *Real repentance is something more than "I'm sorry I got caught," or "I'm sorry I tasted the fruit, because I didn't like the flavor."*

8. What does this verse indicate is the purpose of this confession and prayer?

Digging Deeper

To one degree or another, we all fall into the trap of comparing ourselves with others. We want to appear spiritual in our own eyes, and so we look for someone to feel superior to. Sometimes we forget that God sees right through our pretensions to the "Real Me," with all its ugliness and problems. Read **Luke 18:9–14.** What would a "Pharisee prayer" be in your life? What would a "sinner's prayer" be?

Ponder and Pray

Have you ever had anyone apologize to you with the "I'm sorry, but you . . ." line? If we were honest, we'd all have to say, "Not only heard it, I've done it!" We all do it, and we all know just how "un-sorry" it is. For an example of a real prayer of repentance, read **Psalm 38.** Have you humbled yourself before God to this extent?

Bonus Activity

Read **Colossians 3:5–17** this week. Consider how you can "put off the old" and "put on the new" in your life.

Crying Out
for Forgiveness:
God Offers Hope

When we have taken a good, hard look at ourselves "with
the light on," what we see can be pretty discouraging.
Sometimes the things the Lord brings up are a complete
shock. We hadn't looked at them the way He does. It is
hard to realize that we have damaged ourselves and
others by our actions, and we can't undo them. But God
doesn't just leave us hanging with unclean hearts. He
offers us hope for a completely different life.

Five

God Is Merciful

Mercy and truth have met together;
Righteousness and peace have kissed.

PSALM 85:10

Again and again, the Scriptures praise God for His mercy, or as some translations put it, for His *lovingkindness. Lovingkindness* is a word that seems especially lovely and descriptive, showing us the gentle, fatherly quality of God's mercy. Knowing that God is merciful gives us hope to cry out for forgiveness.

Even when we believe and trust in God's mercy, we may still have questions about it. Why does it seem that God says, "No" to us so often? Why do we still have to deal with the aftermath of sins, both our sins and the sins of those around us? I'd like to share a story of two sisters who helped me see the mercy of God from a slightly different angle.

For Laura and Denise, the bond of sisterhood was fragile at best, and their adolescent angst did nothing to help matters. Without the anchor of a stable home and united parents, they floundered around, trying to find a footing. Laura became involved in the church youth group. She committed her life to the Lord and longed to serve Him. Denise went to church, but she didn't like being hemmed in.

Denise wanted to have fun. Laura wanted Denise to be good. They quarreled inevitably and often. By the time Laura left for college, they really didn't have much to say to each other. Denise had firmly rejected Laura's lifestyle and the morals she had been taught as a child. She wanted to go her own way, and Laura realized that she had to let her go.

More mature now, Laura prayed for her sister, loved her, and tried to build up their relationship. "I was being kind of legalistic," she realized as she reflected on her teenaged arguments with her sister. Denise only saw rules and control, and she wanted to run her own life. She wanted to have her own kind of fun, and she wanted none of this religious bondage, goody-two-shoes stuff.

Not too surprisingly, Denise's actions caught up with her and she became pregnant just after she graduated from high school. Though it was not convenient, she did not even consider abortion. In spite of her rebellion, Denise had no doubt of what God would think about such a step. She decided to keep the baby.

Laura was saddened and concerned, but in a way she was relieved as well. Denise's decision to keep her baby, and a new thoughtfulness she was showing, seemed so encouraging. She began to be excited about being an aunt, and communicated her joy and support to Denise. Now that she was going to be a mother, Denise began to reach out to her sister again. Laura went to the hospital with her, and had the joy of welcoming her niece, Lilly, into the world. They each loved Lilly so much that they were drawn closer together than ever before.

Some months later, Laura and Denise were sharing an afternoon together with Lilly. As they watched her playing, Denise said, "You know, Laura, I used to think that God was a spoilsport—that He was just mean and didn't want me to have a good time. But I'm finding something out. It is really hard to be a single parent. It is going to be really hard to raise Lilly all by myself. I think now that God gives us limits because He wanted to spare me, not because He didn't want me to have a good time."

It was God's mercy that had given Denise limits. Denise had sinned, and she was bearing the consequences of that sin. But God is merciful to us after we disobey, as well as before. Yes, it would be hard to raise Lilly alone, but Lilly would be a joy and delight to her, a good gift that God gave her in spite of her rebellion.

We have learned of God's holiness and justice. We know that He will not tolerate sin, and also that we are all sinners. It would be easy to view His judgments as harsh or unfair, because after all, who enjoys punishment? But let's look beyond our initial rejection and consider a deeper question of who God really is, and why He gives us the limits that we find so hard to take.

1. Read *Hebrews 12:5–11.* In what way could chastening or discipline be a way of showing love?

2. Do you feel loved when things are not going well for you? Is feeling loved as important as being loved? Is there a difference?

When I was a teenager, I had a music teacher who was a very forthright woman. I found her unnerving when I first met her, but as time went on, I began to find that her straightforward style was more useful to me than any of my gentler, more "encouraging" teachers. Mrs. Wilson would say right out, "That was awful!" She pointed out mistakes and flaws that I didn't even know existed. Through her just criticisms, I became aware of my music in much greater detail and at a much deeper level than ever before. But she didn't stop there. Even though she showed me where I was wrong, she also taught me how to repair my mistakes and improve my technique. Because she helped me, I was assured that her criticism was for my good. Because she would honestly tell me when I was awful, I could believe her when she said, "Well done!"

3. Do you ever feel "picked on" by your life circumstances? In what way do you think these problems may be designed for your growth?

4. What is the fruit of being chastened or punished? Is this fruit inevitable, or does it depend on your response?

5. If we sin but repent sincerely, why do we still have to bear the consequences?

6. Why do parents discipline their children? What would you say about a parent who ignored a child's misbehavior?

7. *As the writer of Hebrews points out, no one enjoys being chastened or disciplined. Dealing with the consequences of our sins can be so daunting that we begin to feel that we cannot bear it. But God is not only just, He is merciful. He lets us bear trouble to build us up, not to tear us down. Read* **Psalm 36:5–9.** *How big is God's mercy? What does it provide for us?*

Let's look beyond our initial rejection and consider a deeper question of who God really is, and why He gives us the limits that we find so hard to take.

8. *What is the connection between God's mercy, and His faithfulness, righteousness, and judgment? How does knowing about the mercy of God speak to you about hope for forgiveness?*

Digging Deeper

Think about the most difficult trial you have faced in your life. Where can you see God's chastening? Where can you see His mercy? What growth has occurred in your life as a result?

Ponder and Pray

Read **Psalm 85:10** and **Psalm 89:14** and contemplate on these verses. What do they tell you about God's character of mercy? What about His character of judgment?

Bonus Activity

The great thing about God's mercy is that it never runs out. In fact, His Word tells us that God's mercies are "new every morning" (see **Lamentations 3:23–25**). Every morning this week, take time to thank God for His new mercies.

Six

Forgive Me!

Have mercy upon me, O God,
According to Your lovingkindness;
According to the multitude of Your tender mercies,
Blot out my transgressions

PSALM 51:1

Did you know that forgiveness is something you have to want in order to receive? In order for forgiveness to result in restoration and healing, it has to be a two-way street. Sometimes we won't let ourselves desire forgiveness. We are too proud to admit that we need it; we don't want to be humbled enough to say, "I blew it. I don't deserve anything. Please forgive me."

Jesus told a story that beautifully illustrates the concept of asking for forgiveness. He described a man who had two sons. The younger son wanted to have some fun in life, so he asked to have his inheritance given to him immediately. He didn't want to stay home and work on Dad's farm, and inherit half of it when he was too old to enjoy it. He wanted to have his fling immediately.

So his father divided up his assets. Jesus didn't say why the father chose to give in to his son's whim. Maybe he wanted his son to decide to stay home out of love, not by being forced to. Whatever the reason, he did it, and the younger son hit the road as soon as the cash was in his pocket. He went to a far country and proceeded to spend his inheritance on wild living. It probably seemed like a lot of fun at first. No one to tell him what to do, no work, plenty of wine, women, and parties. Then the blow fell. The money ran out and his friends deserted him. Finally he got so hungry that he took a job feeding pigs. Remember, he would have been raised to consider pigs as unclean animals, and here he was feeding them! He got so desperate that he would have started eating pig feed if he had been able to digest it.

It was while he was in distress and hunger that God finally got his attention. He realized suddenly that even his father's lowest servants were better off than he was. He decided to go home. Here is the important part of his story. He didn't decide to go home and sponge off of Dad. He wasn't expecting any mercy. He just thought that even if he had to work as a slave to stay alive, he'd rather work for his father where he'd at least be fed. He must have known that his father was a fair master. He planned out what he would say: *"Father, I have sinned against heaven and before you, and I am no longer worthy to be called your son. Make me like one of your hired servants."*

He went home, hoping for nothing better than a job that would feed and shelter him. But he had underestimated his father.

Even from a distance, his father recognized him. He saw the pitiful state he was in, and his heart was filled with compassion for his lost son. The father ran to meet him, wrapping his arms around him, overjoyed.

I'm sure the son was overcome by this loving greeting, but he didn't try to pretend that he was any better than he was. He told his father just what he had planned to tell him: that he had sinned terribly and was only hoping for a job. He knew that he deserved nothing—he had already taken his inheritance from his father, and spent it all. He was asking for only a little mercy.

His father's response must have dazed and amazed him. Instead of rebuking him for having wasted his inheritance or telling him what a bum he was, his father called for his best clothes and planned a party. *"For this my son was dead and is alive again; he was lost and is found"* (read **Luke 15:11–31**).

This beautiful story of repentance and forgiveness is a clear picture of God's love and forgiveness for us. The father was ready to forgive the son, and eager to do so. But in order to receive the father's forgiveness, the son had to come home. He had to humbly make the journey back to the place where he went wrong. It wouldn't have done the son a bit of good for his father to write and tell him, "I forgive you" while he was in the midst of his riotous living. Someone who is enjoying sin is not interested in forgiveness. No need is felt. Long distance forgiveness could not have restored the son to his place in the father's household. He had removed himself from the father's household, and nothing the father said about forgiveness could change that fact. The father had forgiveness and restoration waiting, but it could not be given until the son returned.

1. *Read **Acts 5:31**. What is the connection between repentance and forgiveness? Can a person who has not repented be forgiven? Why or why not?*

2. Can a person who has not repented be restored? Why or why not?

3. Is there a difference between forgiveness and restoration? Does true forgiveness necessarily include restoration?

4. Read **Acts 11:18.** According to this verse, what is the result of repentance? What does this mean?

5. *Earlier we talked about* **1 John 1:9**. *What is important about confession? How does it connect with repentance and forgiveness?*

While we do have to come to God for forgiveness, there is no set formula or prayer that we have to get right in order to obtain forgiveness. God is interested in our hearts, not in recited words. He desires a relationship with us, not just a business transaction.

6. *Read* **Luke 23:39–43**. *What tells you that the second criminal was repentant, not just sorry he was caught? How did he ask for forgiveness?*

7. *Read Acts 16:25–34. What tells you that the jailer was repentant? How did he ask for forgiveness?*

In order to receive forgiveness, we have to want it.

8. *What do these stories tell you about how to ask for forgiveness? What is the bottom line?*

Digging Deeper

Do you think that the jailer would have needed to be more specific in his repentance later on, as he grew in the Lord? Why or why not? Of what use is specific repentance?

Ponder and Pray

King David is described in Scripture as a "man after God's own heart," but that does not mean that he was perfect. In fact, he did some dreadful things. But when he recognized his sin, he was truly repentant. Read **Psalm 51** and think about how David asked for forgiveness. How did he describe his sin? What did he beg for again and again? What does this show you about how he viewed the importance of his relationship with God?

Bonus Activity

Work on memorizing **Matthew 7:7–8** this week. Do you believe that if you ask for forgiveness, you will find it?

Seven

God Seeks Sinners

*For the Son of Man has come to seek and to save
that which was lost.*

Luke 19:10

Have you ever tried to find something you've lost? Maybe it was car keys or important papers, your favorite shirt or the CD you used to listen to all the time. You may lose your way occasionally. You may have even had the terrible experience of losing track of your child, and remember searching frantically through a crowd trying to find him or her.

Searching for something lost has such a core connection to us that a search or quest is often a part of the most enduring of fictional stories. One such search is described in the old classic novel *David Copperfield*.

Little Emily was a pretty girl, brought up by her kind foster father, Mr. Peggotty. Mr. Peggotty was a poor working man, who had taken Emily in when her own parents died. He loved her as his own daughter, and never thought of her as anything else. Emily grew up loving Mr. Peggotty and his son, and yet longing for something more exciting than the poor life they lived. When she was a young woman, engaged to a fine, gentle young man she had known all her life, Emily's life was disrupted by the arrival of a handsome, charming, wealthy young gentleman. He greatly admired her beauty, and having nothing else to occupy his time, he set out to seduce her. Eventually, the temptation was too great, and believing (or hoping) that he would marry her, Emily ran away with the young man. She knew that her action would destroy her reputation, and cause pain to her family, but she comforted herself with the thought that when she was married, she would be rich and able to help their poverty.

Her fiancé and her foster father were heartbroken. They knew what kind of man she had run away with, and knew that he would not marry her. Emily had not only betrayed her family, she was completely ruined. In that era, a girl with that kind of stain on her reputation would never be accepted into the community again. She had branded herself a harlot, and she had brought shame to the man who had carefully raised her.

No one would have been surprised, or blamed Mr. Peggotty in the least if he had disowned Emily. After all, she was only an adopted child, not really his responsibility. In the society she came from, she had done the unforgivable. But Mr. Peggotty did not only see Emily's sin. He thought of Emily, and the heartbreak and shame that she would feel when the rich young man abandoned her. He knew that she would never return home when she realized what she had done. She would be too ashamed. If he did not care for her, she would sink into deeper and deeper sin and degradation. So he set out in search of her. He went on foot—he could afford nothing else—and he searched for many months. When he finally found her, she was afraid at first to see him and hid her face. But Mr. Peggotty had not been searching for her in order to repudiate her. He searched for her because he loved her, and longed for her to be restored. Like the father of the prodigal son, he gathered her in his arms, and rejoiced that she was found.

We have learned that God is just, and that sin cannot be overlooked. We have learned that He is merciful, and that His purpose is always to work for our good. We have also learned that God is ready to forgive, just as the father was ready to forgive his wayward son. The picture of that father running to meet his child touches our hearts deeply, but it gets even better. God is not only willing to forgive and restore sinners, He actively seeks the unworthy to bring them back to His family. He goes out looking for the lost, just like Mr. Peggotty went looking for little Emily.

1. *The image of the Lord as our shepherd is used again and again to describe His tender, watchful care for us. Read* **Isaiah 40:10–11** *and* **Psalm 23**. *In a few words, what characteristics of God do these passages show?*

2. *In teaching His disciples, Jesus also refers to Himself as the Good Shepherd. Read* **John 10:11–16**. *What does this passage add to the picture of God as Shepherd?*

3. Who are the "sheep not of this fold"? How will Jesus bring them into the flock?

4. Read **Luke 15:1–7**. How does this story answer the Pharisees' criticism? Why is Jesus so interested in sinners, and not in the people who are trying to be good?

5. How far does the Lord go in seeking sinners?

6. One of the most amazing stories of God's pursuing love is the story of Paul (or Saul), the fiery saint who started out persecuting believers, and who ended up planting churches all over the Roman Empire and dying in prison for the sake of Christ. Read *Acts 9:1–19*. What seems like the most astonishing part of this story?

_____

> *God is not only willing to forgive and restore sinners, He actively seeks the unworthy to bring them back to His family.*

_____

7. Notice how Saul addresses the voice and the bright light in verse 5. What might this suggest about who Saul thinks it is?

8. *Most of us probably don't see a goad often in our everyday life, but Saul would have been very familiar with this tool. A goad is a sharp pointed stick, used to poke an ox in the right direction when he is acting up. What do you think the Lord was saying to Saul when He said, "It is hard for you to kick against the goads"?*

9. *What behavior indicates that Saul had repented and turned in the opposite direction?*

Digging Deeper

Some of us have dramatic stories. Some of us moved more quietly into a relationship with God. In your journey to becoming a Christ follower, what alerted you to your need for God? How did you find Him? Read **Luke 19:1–10** for a story of Jesus seeking sinners, and how it resulted in a life-changing event.

Ponder and Pray

While we rejoice over God's seeking and pursuing love, let's not forget what it cost Him to come after us. Read **Luke 22:39–45** and **23:26–49**. Remembering the suffering and death of Christ keeps alive for us the reality of His love.

Bonus Activity

This week, seek out a friend whom you can ask about their salvation story, and tell them yours. Take time to thank God together for seeking out each one of us.

Eight

For a Worthless Sinner?

We love Him because He first loved us.

1 JOHN 4:19

Recently our neighborhood had its annual Community Rummage Sale. These are always interesting events—baked goods, lunch, and enormous quantities of "rummage," all for bargain prices. The junk is just about what anyone would expect. There is the usual selection of clothing: out of fashion (way out!), or size 2 (and how long has it been since we were that small?), or just a little too dingy. The overstuffed chairs have obviously been dredged up from basements, with the color selection ranging mostly from faded avocado to orange polyester tweed. The pots and pans are all aluminum, and quite dented. The dishes range from scratched Corelle to someone's collection of souvenir coffee mugs that say "I ❤ Panama City." Occasionally you run across a great bargain, like an almost new kitchen range, a set of bunk beds, or a twin stroller. Sometimes you'll find a brand-new shirt—just your size—or a set of water glasses to replace those that finally broke.

This year my mother's find was an oak rocking chair. It was sitting there, albeit crookedly, for the very reasonable price of five dollars. It didn't look particularly appealing at first glance, but my mother likes rocking chairs, and she noticed that it had been built in a cute, older style. Broken up, it wasn't worth much, but if she repaired it, it could be a lovely chair. My parents took it home, and since it was in his way, my father started fixing it up right away. He took the old rocker off and threw it in the stove, and he built a strong, solid new one in its place. When the chair was all fixed, we discovered that it was not only an attractive piece of furniture, but it was also extremely comfortable. The chair that was on its way to the junk heap is now the inhabitant of a cozy living room.

My parents didn't save the rocker because they were so desperate for furniture that they would take any old piece of junk. Nor did they save it because they had to—they had no responsibility for the chair. They saved it because they saw its potential, and thought it was worth rescuing. They thought it was too good a chair to be thrown away when it could be repaired and made beautiful and useful again.

"Amazing Grace," one of the most beloved of all hymns, was written by a man who fully understood sin and degradation. John Newton had been the captain of a slave ship, and he was guilty of the worst cruelties to his fellow humans. When God convicted John of his sin, he repented with great sorrow. His repentance and his realization of his wickedness are clearly pictured in his hymn:

> *Amazing grace, how sweet the sound*
> *That saved a wretch like me!*
> *I once was lost, but now am found*
> *Was blind, but now I see.*

Conviction of guilt is painful. We don't like to consider ourselves wretches or worms, and it seems that we usually deal with this in one of two ways. Either we want to deny the fact that we are sinners, making excuses for ourselves and explaining away what we have done; or we simply wallow in our wretchedness. We believe that we are too ugly and repulsive for anyone to care for, and we just lie down and moan about our unworthiness. It seems that we either refuse the gift of salvation because we think we don't need it, or we refuse it because we think we're not worth it.

The truth is that we certainly are not worthy of salvation. That is made completely clear by a simple exploration of God's justice and holiness. In fact, it is our very unworthiness that makes us candidates for salvation. Someone who is already perfect doesn't need help.

We are not worthy. But God has made it clear that we are worth it to Him. He didn't make the sacrifice because someone else made Him do it, or because He was desperate for company in heaven. He did it because He wanted to. He is love, and He loved us. He gave the ultimate love-gift to the human race: His own Son. "Greater love has no one than this, than to lay down one's life for his friends" (John 15:13).

Knowledge of our sin should fill us with sorrow, as we see how we have cut ourselves off from God. Our sins are what nailed Jesus to the cross, and brought Him to tears and anguish. But we should be filled with a sorrow that leads to repentance and change, not despair, because we know that our sins didn't make Him throw us away. God wanted us to be in a right relationship with Him so much that He was willing to pay the price. And no one pays a high price for something that he or she considers worthless. He saved us because He could see our potential, and thought we were worth rescuing.

1. Read **Romans 5:6–8**. What does the phrase "still without strength" refer to? Do we have strength now?

2. What is the difference between a righteous man and a good man? What might make you willing to die for someone else?

3. Are we deserving of Christ's sacrifice? Why or why not? Why did He do it?

4. Read **Hebrews 12:1–2**. What does it mean to say that Jesus is both "author" and "finisher" of our faith?

5. Why did Jesus die on the cross? What was the joy set before Him?

_____

> **God wanted us to be in right relationship with Him so much that He was willing to pay the price.**

_____

6. Read **1 Peter 2:24–25**. What did it cost Jesus to pay for our sins? Do you think this was easy for Him? Read **Luke 22:39–46**.

7. Do you ever find it difficult to feel that Jesus was or is really interested in you personally? Read **John 17:20–26**. Who was He praying for? How does it apply to you?

8. How has God demonstrated His love for you?

Digging Deeper

Read all of **Isaiah 53**. Whom is this passage talking about? Read verses 10–12 again. Why did this Servant of God suffer? What were the results of this suffering? How does this apply to you?

Ponder and Pray

The apostle John talks more about love than any other New Testament writer. He often describes himself in the Gospel of John as "the disciple whom Jesus loved." Obviously, he felt a deep connection to the Lord, and really understood the love that Jesus has for fallen humans. Read **1 John 4:7–21**. What did John have to say about God's love? How does this love affect us, both eternally and presently?

Bonus Activity

What is some special way that you can show your loved ones that you think they are worth loving? Think of a service that you can do for someone special to you sometime this week—take some extra time to really show this person that you care. Here are some examples of things you could do:

- Write a note
- Do a chore
- Lift a burden
- Give a hug
- Fix a treat
- Go on an outing
- Make a gift
- Listen

Embracing the Power of Forgiveness

God's forgiveness is not just some legal transaction, letting us "off the hook." Instead, God's forgiveness is a life-changing power. When God forgives, He goes all the way.

God is our River of Life. He intends that His living water should not only quench our spiritual thirst, but should also cleanse us and then flow through us. God doesn't spot clean with a cotton swab. He opens the fire hydrant of life and love and leaves it running.

Nine

God's Forgiveness Is Complete: He Brings Restoration

In Him we have redemption through His blood,
the forgiveness of sins, according
to the riches of His grace.

EPHESIANS 1:7

The acquisition and preservation of antiques, original artwork, and other such museum-worthy artifacts is an absorbing subject. The first step for any collector is, of course, to find and purchase the items worth preserving. The work of many wealthy art connoisseurs has preserved for the world the great art of the ages. Paintings and sculptures that might otherwise have been lost have been saved by these people, who hunt the world for beautiful objects.

At first glance, this may seem to be adequate. The mere fact that these items have been kept safe means that they are available to be admired and appreciated by future generations. But really dedicated collectors of artifacts go a step further. They not only redeem the artwork from being lost, they also set about to restore it to its former beauty. Ancient paintings that have become dingy with accumulated centuries of dust, dirt, candle smoke, coal smog, and darkening varnish are carefully cleaned so that the original is revealed as the artist actually meant it to be. Tattered manuscripts are carefully mended and copied. Shattered sculptures are delicately pieced together. When the famous ceiling of the Sistine Chapel was cleaned, the world was amazed at the brilliance of Michelangelo's original painting. It took twelve years of slow, painstaking work, but in the end, it was worth it. Even dingy and dark, the Sistine Chapel was amazing. Seen in its original colors, it became fantastic.

The word *restoration* is used in another sense as well. The Sistine Chapel was "restored" in that it was brought back to its original state. A great work of art could also be "restored" by returning it to its original owner. During the Second World War, a great number of famous works of art were stolen by the Nazis. Some were lost, but after the war, many of them were restored to the countries from which they had been taken. For these works of art, their restoration meant that they were brought home.

The restoration of these famous works of art is a picture of the way God handles us. God not only redeems us, paying for us so that we will not be destroyed. He also cleanses us, restoring us to our original beauty. Our sins are like the years of dirt and scum that darken and obscure a beautiful painting, but God, as our Creator, sees beneath it all. He knows exactly what He really meant this picture to look like, and so His restoration is perfect. And not only does He cleanse us and make us like new, He also brings us home, restored to our original owner. God's forgiveness is complete.

We long for forgiveness and restoration, but in order to be able to receive it, we need to believe that God is actually able to forgive our sins.

1. Read **Mark 2:1–12**. In verse 10, some translations use the word power in this passage, and some use the word authority. What is the difference between power and authority? In what way do both of these words help you understand Jesus?

2. What gave Jesus the power/authority to forgive sins? Would it do you any good to be forgiven by someone who did not have this power or authority? Why or why not?

3. Read **Luke 24:44–47**. Why was it necessary for Jesus to suffer and die, and also to be raised from the dead?

4. What is the "remission of sins"? How is it connected to repentance?

Do you remember how the father responded to his lost son? He not only offered forgiveness, in terms of not punishing him or reproaching him, but he also put his son back into the position he had thrown away. The father's forgiveness brought about reconciliation, a restoration to the way things were before the son's rebellion had broken the relationship.

*5. Read **Romans 5:9–11**. What is the result of being justified (declared righteous)? What does this mean?*

Not only does God cleanse us and make us like new, He also brings us home, restored to our original owner.

6. What does it mean to be reconciled to God? What does this look like?

Human beings have a strong, innate knowledge that we are "not quite right." We are constantly longing for something better, something to explain the dissatisfaction and trouble we have with life. It is as though we have a deep, hidden memory of the time when humans were in right relationship with God, and we are drawn to it, longing to get back the sense of rightness that we have never had. Many so-called primitive cultures have their own legends of how they lost contact with the Creator. Modern "civilized" culture has rejected these legends, as well as the true account in Genesis, but we still feel the need to be set right.

*7. Read **Genesis 3:8–9; 22–24**. What clues do these verses give you about how God originally designed humans to relate to Him? What changed when Adam and Eve rebelled and ate the forbidden fruit?*

8. Read **Galatians 4:4–7**. What is the purpose of God's forgiveness? What does it mean to be an heir of Christ?

Digging Deeper

God's forgiveness and restoration is complete, down to the last detail. Read **Revelation 22:1–5**. How do these verses parallel the account in Genesis? What is the significance of the tree of life in the two accounts?

Ponder and Pray

God's relationship with rebellious Israel gives us an amazing picture of His love for sinners. Read **Hosea 11:1–11** and **14:1–9**. How has God shown His love for you? When has He shown you forbearance? What restoration has He accomplished in your life?

Bonus Activity

There is something comforting about restoring an object that has been damaged. In a small way, it is a picture of the restoration that God is working in our lives. This week, take time to restore order to a corner of your life—even just a drawer or closet or box of junk. Reflect on God's restoration, and thank Him for His love.

Ten

Embracing Forgiveness

If the Son makes you free,
you shall be free indeed.

JOHN 8:36

Jeannie found it hard to describe how things had seemed to her, or to understand why she felt the way she did. For some reason, she had struggled all through her childhood with feelings of rebellion, depression, and insecurity. While her parents were certainly not perfect, they were loving and sincere in their desire to raise their children to follow the Lord. Jeannie's unhappiness worried them very much, especially as they saw her take out her feelings on her younger siblings. While they did have some good times together, unfortunately Jeannie's ruling attitude was one of scorn and derision for her family. If they annoyed her, she let them know it in a screech. She ridiculed them, sometimes in public, and generally made their lives difficult. Each of her siblings handled this differently, sometimes purposely pushing her buttons to see her steam, sometimes ignoring her completely, sometimes trying to please her. Jeannie could be fun and funny when she was in a good mood, but her moods ruled, and they learned to watch for them.

Jeannie's rebellion went the way that rebellion does, and her teenage years were stormy and full of things that she deeply regretted later. But her family never stopped caring or praying for her, and after Jeannie grew up, she found the Lord. Just as her parents had prayed, her life was turned around. Jeannie's family watched in joy and amazement as they saw the change come over her. As Jeannie embraced God's forgiveness, she began to "clean house" and work on rebuilding what she had broken. She began to tell the people she had wounded with her meanness just how sorry she was, and to ask for forgiveness. She repented of her rebellion, and the stupid and wrong things she had done when she rejected her parents.

As her family watched, they were thrilled to find that this new Jeannie seemed more like the "real Jeannie" than she ever had in her life. She was so different, and yet she was more herself than she had ever been. God's forgiveness had set Jeannie free indeed.

Jeannie's freedom came about because she was willing to accept and embrace God's forgiveness. It seems so easy and obvious, but in fact, we often find it hard to embrace forgiveness. Sometimes we don't want to admit that we need it. Other times, we know our need, but we fear that God can't or won't really forgive. We can't believe that we can be cleansed and start again.

God offers forgiveness freely, but we have to embrace it into our lives in order for His power to work in us. Think about the story of the lost son again. When the father showed his love and forgiveness, the son did not say, "No thanks, Dad. You don't really want to forgive me. You obviously don't understand. You can't love me anymore. Just show me the way to the nearest pigpen." Instead, he accepted his father's gift, and put on the new clothes and ate the food provided.

God's forgiveness makes all things new. Don't dwell on past failures. Instead, take up the new life He offers and build again.

1. Read **Philippians 3:13–14.** What is ahead of us?

2. What is behind you? What kinds of "things which are behind" do you find hardest to forget?

3. When we still have reminders and consequences of our past sins in our lives, it is very hard to "forget" them and move forward. We know that we can't will ourselves to completely forget our pasts. So what does this passage mean? What should we forget? Is there any value in remembering your past sins?

4. Read **Psalm 23:3**. What is a restored soul? What seems to accompany a restored soul? Why?

5. Read **John 5:5–9, 24**; and **John 8:10–11**. Both of these people experienced a remarkable encounter with the Savior. What response did Jesus tell them they should give? What is the significance of this?

Some of us have struggled with pride, not wanting to admit our own neediness before the Lord. Taking a good look at who He is, and measuring ourselves against that, has to pretty well eliminate that kind of self-satisfaction. But sometimes this leads us down the other path, to the point where we despair of being forgiven because our sins are so great. Be comforted as you read of a great sinner and a great forgiveness.

6. Read **Luke 22:54–62**. Why did Peter deny Jesus? What was the significance of Jesus' looking at him?

> *God's forgiveness makes all things new. Don't dwell on past failures. Instead, take up the new life He offers and build again.*

7. Read **John 21:15–19**. What was Jesus saying to Peter? How did Peter respond? (For more details of Peter's subsequent life and actions, see Acts 2–4.)

8. What might embracing forgiveness look like in your life?

Digging Deeper

Read **2 Corinthians 5:17**. How can you be "in Christ"? What does it mean to be a new creation? (See also **John 3:1–8**).

Ponder and Pray

Grief for sins committed and regret for what might have been are hard to bear. It is true that we cannot undo the past, and sometimes the consequences of our sins linger for a long time—even for our whole lives. But God is able to work these bad things for good in our lives, if we will let Him, and even to restore goodness that we have completely missed in our times of rebellion and disobedience. Read **Joel 2:25**. What have the "locusts eaten" in your life? Have you prayed for the Lord to restore you?

Bonus Activity

Read **Psalm 103:1–5**, and join the psalmist in praising God for His forgiveness and healing.

Eleven

The Clean Slate

You will cast all our sins into the depths of the sea.

MICAH 7:19

Unfortunately, mother-in-law trouble is something a large percentage of young wives have to deal with. Probably most mothers never imagine that they will be difficult mothers-in-law. But when their darling sons marry, and suddenly Mom's importance is overshadowed, many mothers take out their frustrations on their daughters-in-law. They criticize and tear down where they should be encouraging and building up. Sometimes they create irreparable relationship damage.

This was what happened between Jenny and her mother-in-law, Marlene. Although she had initially expressed joy over her son's marriage, and was warm and friendly to Jenny, Marlene had a bad habit of oversensitivity, and worse, she was a grudge-bearer. Soon, Jenny began to find that she was constantly offending Marlene, or hurting her feelings in some way. At first, this concerned Jenny, and she tried to make things right. She would apologize to Marlene, and work hard to smooth things over and keep her happy. But it seemed that nothing was ever really fixed. No matter what Jenny did to make amends, Marlene did not forget the past. Every real or imagined slight was stored up and carefully saved, to fuel her hurt whenever she was again offended with Jenny. She would say that she forgave her, but they were never able to start over again with a clean slate.

Susie's problems with her mother-in-law, Rebecca, were similar to Jenny's problems in some ways, but with a significant difference.

Rebecca was often very critical of Susie. She was insensitive to Susie's needs as a new wife who was still unsure of her role. Rebecca did many things that hurt Susie deeply. Like Marlene, Rebecca tended to be controlling, and had a difficult time letting go of her adult children. As the first daughter-in-law, Susie had a lot to deal with. But Rebecca had one characteristic that made Susie's problems very different from Jenny's problems. Rebecca was able to forget. She had had a very traumatic and abusive upbringing, and in order to cope with it, she had made a habit of living very much in and for the present. Once the emotions of a conflict had passed, Rebecca let the whole thing go as water under the bridge. By not bearing a grudge, Rebecca and Susie were able to build a mother- and daughter-in-law relationship centered on love and forgiveness.

Most of us have had experiences with both kinds of life conflict—dealing with the grudge-bearer, and with the one who simply ignores a past battle and expects to move right on. We know that neither one is an adequate way to handle disagreements and hurts that we have caused each other. Even when the words "I forgive you" were spoken, Marlene's grudges were nothing more or less than basic unforgiveness. Rebecca's forgetfulness left Susie with all the burden of forgiveness on her side, because there was never any acknowledgment of the problems. Whoever was in the wrong, never addressing it left Susie having to deal with all the aftermath alone.

Our human version of forgiveness often falls wide of the mark, but God's forgiveness never fails. He doesn't pretend that nothing ever happened, nor does He leave us alone to deal with all the bad feelings left over from our sins. Neither does He "forgive" and then still hold it against us. Instead, God's forgiveness is all about cleansing. When you are forgiven by God, you get a clean slate. You start again, fresh. A few weeks ago, we read from 1 John 1:9 that when we confess our sins, God is "faithful and just to forgive us our sins, and to cleanse us from all unrighteousness." Read that verse again, just to get the feel of it. From God, forgiveness and cleansing go hand in hand.

1. Read **Psalm 103:11–14.** *Poetically speaking, how far is the east from the west? How can God remove our transgressions?*

2. *In light of this verse, could a person who had fewer sins to be forgiven be considered more valuable or special or worthy?*

3. How does a father "pity his children"? What is the significance of God knowing our frame and remembering our dustiness?

In C. S. Lewis's *The Lion, The Witch and the Wardrobe,* the boy Edmund starts out as a particularly unpleasant little pill. In order to get more of the witch's enchanted candy, he plans to betray his own siblings and the whole land of Narnia. He had joined the losing side, however, and nearly perished at the hands of the witch. At the last moment, he was rescued from certain death and brought before Aslan. He had to stand there as an utter failure, with the sickening realization of what he had done. He was not only a traitor; he wasn't even successful in his treachery. He had to be rescued by those he had professed to despise. To make matters worse, as a traitor, he now legally belonged to the witch. By rights, Aslan should have turned from him in disgust, and let the witch kill him. Instead, he freely offered to forgive Edmund and to take his place as the witch's sacrifice.

Edmund was such a stinker at the beginning that you might wonder how the others could forgive what he had tried to do. You might think that at the very least he would be placed on probation, to prove that he was really on the right side now. Instead, he was given a sword to fight Aslan's enemies, and given the place of a son, along with the others. Even though he started out with a chip on his shoulder, Edmund turned into a hero. Because he had been forgiven much, he was able to do great things.

4. Read **Luke 7:36–48**. What was this woman doing? Why didn't Jesus seem to care that she was a woman with such a bad reputation?

5. What was the big difference between Simon and the woman in their reactions to Jesus? How does this relate to how much they needed to be forgiven?

6. Why might someone with a heavier load of sin have a better understanding of forgiveness?

7. *God's forgiveness means restoration, cleansing, and a new start in life. But we still have to step forward and take the new beginning. Read the apostle Paul's wake-up call in* **Romans 6:1–11.** *How does baptism illustrate Christ's death and resurrection?*

8. *What did Christ's death accomplish for us? What does His resurrection accomplish?*

> *From God,*
> *forgiveness and*
> *cleansing go hand*
> *in hand.*

9. *How can God give us a clean slate? What does it mean to be "alive to God" or to "live with Him"?*

Digging Deeper

Read **Hebrews 10:14.** What is this verse saying? Some have read this verse and believed that we can reach perfection here in this life. What do you think of this thought? What might it mean to be "perfected forever"? Discuss the interesting juxtaposition of "perfected forever" and "being sanctified."

Ponder and Pray

To review what we have learned about forgiveness, reread the opening verse at the head of each chapter. Have you asked for forgiveness? Have you embraced the forgiveness God offers?

Bonus Activity

Memorize this chapter's opening verse. Say or sing this old children's Sunday school song:

Jesus took my burdens, and He rolled them in the sea,
Never to remember anymore.

Twelve

Forgive As You Have Been Forgiven

And forgive us our debts, as we forgive our debtors.

MATTHEW 6:12

When I was a girl, I helped out with Vacation Bible School as a "big kid." One day one of the teachers told a story that I have never forgotten. Our teacher, Constance, had with her two pans of red Jell-O. One pan she had made the day before, extra stiff. It was cold and hard. The second pan she mixed together seconds before the lesson began, so it was warm and liquid. She let the children come and stick their fingers in the two pans of Jell-O before the lesson started, and the kids had a great time making big jabs into the smooth, stiff Jell-O, and swirling the liquid Jell-O around the pan. Then she told her story.

In junior high school, she told us, there was one girl who seemed to make it her specialty to pick on her at every opportunity. When Constance passed her in the hall, this girl, Trudy, would stop and look Constance up and down, slowly from top to toe. She'd say, sneering,

"Nice shoes you've got, Thompson," and then move up a fraction, "Nice socks you've got, Thompson," and so on, until she had ridiculed everything about Constance's appearance. Then Trudy would saunter off with her friends, well satisfied with her wit. It was the most withering experience, and Constance understandably resented her.

It was around this time that Constance also found the Lord. Her heart went out to the Savior, and she embraced Him wholeheartedly, determined to live her life His way. Over the next few years, God was faithful to His promises, and Constance continued to grow and to know Him more. To her relief, she and Trudy had parted ways by high school, and she was able to forget her scorn and derision. Constance entered nursing school, graduated as an RN, and began working in a large hospital. She loved her work, and her buoyant enthusiasm was an encouragement to co-workers and patients alike. Often the more experienced nurses were expected to chaperone the new LPNs and show them their way around, and Constance enjoyed this as well.

Imagine Constance's consternation when she recognized her old nemesis, Trudy, among the new recruits one day. She couldn't help but imagine how their dreaded meeting would go down: the long, insolent stare, and the derisive comment of "Nice uniform, Thompson." But to her astonishment, nothing like this happened. In fact, Trudy did not appear to even recognize or remember her. To make matters even more peculiar, she obviously admired Constance, and looked up to her. Constance found that Trudy seemed to think that she was wonderful. There was a real battle of feelings in Constance's heart at this point. While it was sort of gratifying to have their positions reversed, she didn't want to be nice to Trudy. She wanted to be mean to her. She wanted to look her up and down and say, "Nice shoes, Jones," and then saunter away. It was hard to want to forgive. The hurt Trudy had inflicted was still there.

It was at this point that our teacher showed us the two pans of Jell-O again. "My heart was like the cold, set Jell-O," she told us. "When your heart is cold and hard, other people's actions make permanent marks in it, just like your fingers did to this Jell-O. But God wants us to keep our hearts soft, like the second pan of Jell-O. Did you notice, when you put your fingers in that pan, you didn't leave any marks? That's what God wants your heart to be like, so when people hurt you, you can let go and forget it."

God's forgiveness is so great a gift that it demands a response from us. Not to try to earn the gift or to pay God back. That would only be an insult. But if we understand the magnitude of God's gift to us, humility and gratitude demand that we act like we have received it. We want God to forgive us our sins. We must then be willing to forgive the shortcomings of others.

The writer of Hebrews tells us that Jesus became human so that He would be completely able to sympathize with our weaknesses. He was tempted in all points, just as we are, but He resisted to the end and did not sin. Because we know that He understands the limitations of being human, we can come before Him boldly to ask for forgiveness from our sins.

God's kindness to us in His knowledge of our weakness is a precious thing. In the same way we must extend kindness to our fellow humans when they err. We know their weaknesses all too well, for they are the same as our own.

1. Read *John 15:12–14*. *Define what a commandment is. How did Jesus love us? Are you His friend?*

2. Read **Ephesians 4:31–5:2** and **Colossians 3:12–14**. List the behavior we are supposed to eliminate. What do all these words mean?

3. These verses use a number of words to describe the forgiving spirit we must demonstrate: kind, tenderhearted, meek, long-suffering, bearing with, forgiving. Talk about the meaning of each of these words. Give examples of how they might look in "real life."

4. How does God view obedience in this area?

5. *Why is it important to "put on love" or "walk in love"? What do these terms mean?*

Do you remember Jeannie's story? God's forgiveness worked such a change in her heart that she was not only repentant for her rebellion against Him, she also repented of the way she had mistreated others. The first stop in her tour of repentance was her own family. When Jeannie apologized for being a bad big sister, one of her siblings said, "Oh, that's okay. It's no big deal." One of her siblings said, "How can you say that!? You don't realize how much you hurt me!" And one of her siblings said, "Oh, Jeannie, I forgave you a long time ago."

6. *Is the first response Jeannie received true forgiveness? Was it right for Jeannie's sibling to call what she had done "no big deal"? How do you think each of her sibling's responses would affect their future relationships? How do you respond to a confession and request for forgiveness?*

Forgiveness is a subject Jesus addressed at some length with His disciples. He illustrated the terrible importance of forgiveness in the dramatic Parable of the Unmerciful Servant.

7. Read **Matthew 18:21–35**. *Explore Peter's question and Jesus' answer. What if a person keeps doing the exact same thing, again and again? When you get to the 490th time, are you free to stop forgiving? Why or why not?*

> *God's kindness to us in His knowledge of our weakness is a precious thing.*

8. *Was the master obligated to forgive the servant? Why did he do it?*

Digging Deeper

Read **James 2:13.** Also, reread the Lord's Prayer (**Matthew 6:9–15**); **Matthew 18:25; Ephesians 4:32; Colossians 3:13.** Why does God view unforgiveness so seriously? What will be the result of unforgiveness in our lives?

Ponder and Pray

Read **1 John 4:20–21.** What does this mean? Is there anyone whom you have not forgiven? Why? What are you going to do about it?

Bonus Activity

Memorize **Ephesians 4:32.** Repeat this verse to yourself regularly to remind you of how you really want to be.

Leader's Guide

Each chapter begins with an illustration and a short discussion of the topic, to help the women in your group start thinking about the subject at hand and prepare to join in the discussion. Encourage everyone to participate and share their thoughts, even if they are new to Bible study. People learn the most from free and lively discussion, so don't be too quick to "give the right answer." In every study, a number of the questions don't have a simple short answer. Instead, they are designed to help people begin to think more deeply about what the Bible is saying. Encourage participants to bring up more than one view or point for these discussion questions. Don't be afraid to question, or to come to a point where everyone says, "I don't know!" These new questions are the jumping-off point for later in-depth Bible study.

Be sure to give plenty of time for thought as you go through the questions in each chapter. You'll get the best discussion if you are not afraid of moments of silence as you wrestle with difficult questions or new ideas. This guide provides you with some added thoughts to facilitate discussion, or additional references to help you come up with good answers.

The **Focus** restates the main point of each lesson, for your reference as you prepare for the study.

Digging Deeper gives an opportunity to continue an interesting discussion, or dig a little deeper into the subject matter. These questions are optional, but are often useful to round out a study and encourage deeper thinking.

Ponder and Pray usually provides a longer Scripture passage to read and meditate on, as well as bringing up more personal application questions for each participant to consider individually and pray about.

Bonus Activity gives a short, practical application to help you remember what you have learned throughout the following week.

Chapter 1: God Is Light

Focus: *God desires for us to live abundant lives, filled with light and love. He wants us to experience the cleansing power of forgiveness; to be able to see where we are going so that we can move forward with purpose and confidence. And He wants us to not only walk in the light, but to be filled with light.*

1. Think about the attributes of God: love, justice, mercy, holiness, etc., and their opposites.

2. Think about and discuss what happens to darkness when light is present. You can only get rid of darkness in a room by bringing in light, not by chasing out the darkness.

3. Encourage the women to search for the answers to these questions.

4. In talking about condemnation, return to the thoughts of light fellowshiping with darkness. If a person chooses darkness, how can the light reach that person?

5. Also read **John 8:12; 9:5; 12:35; 1 Thessalonians 5:5; Revelation 22:5** and think about them in relation to this question.

6. Coming into the light is a metaphor for coming into a relationship with the Lord.

7. Answers will vary. Encourage people to talk about what makes darkness seem attractive at the moment.

8. Encourage participants to extract the answers to these questions from the passage read. What does the text say? What does it mean?

Chapter 2: Stepping into the Light

Focus: *We can't be free until we are willing to step into the light and see our sins for what they are. Stepping into God's light is the first step to forgiveness and cleansing.*

1. Answers will vary.

2. Answers will vary. Try reciting the Ten Commandments as a group. Don't ask for detailed confession; this question is geared more toward an "on a scale of one to ten" answer.

3. Examples will vary.

4. An important point to note here is how Jesus goes beyond actions to the heart of each of these issues.

5. Encourage participants to come up with examples of the differences. Consider how sins of the heart might lead to sins of action.

6. Answers will vary.

7. Again and again the Bible shows God as wanting to save the lost. Jesus came to earth to actively seek sinners to bring them to repentance.

8. and 9. Encourage participants to explain their answers to these questions, and to question whether their own answers are based on God's Word, or on personal ideas.

Chapter 3: God Is Just

Focus: *God is not only just, He is a savior. That means that He makes a way for sinners, like you and me, to be rescued from the consequences of our sins—not just be "let off the hook."*

1. It might be helpful to bring a dictionary, and look a little deeper at these important words.

2. Justice demands that we pay for our sins, and sins cost death.

3. To "redeem" something is to buy it back. If a person sells something at a pawnshop, and then comes into some money, the person can then "redeem" the item that was sold. When Jesus died on the cross, He paid the price for all our sins, and redeemed us from death.

4. God did not just let our sins go, unjustly ignoring them. Instead, He arranged payment for them. Justice demands that the sins be paid for, mercy allowed someone else to pay the price we could not pay.

5. Only the one to whom the debt is owed can justify the debtor.

6. When we "justify" ourselves, we are only making excuses because we do not have the right to justify. God has the right to justify because He is the one sinned against. Since He is also just, He cannot just say "never mind" about our sins.

7. Forgiveness without cleansing gives no hope for the future.

8. and 9. Encourage participants to give the reasoning behind their answers, and to question what their answers are based on.

Chapter 4: Being Sorry for Sin:
Understanding Repentance

Focus: *Real repentance is something more than "I'm sorry I got caught," or "I'm sorry I tasted the fruit, because I didn't like the flavor." These kinds of "sorry" are certainly real emotions, but they never deal with the heart of the problem. They never deal with the fact that every sin is really a sin against God. Without God's help, we don't have a hope of living in freedom and light.*

1. *Sorrow over sin could also lead to crippling self-pity, anger, depression, or denial.*

2. *The term* godly sorrow *implies that this sorrow reflects some of God's attitude and viewpoint. In contrast, worldly sorrow would reflect the attitude and viewpoint of the world. Encourage discussion on what characterizes these two viewpoints.*

3. *Take enough time on this question to come up with a satisfactory definition of repentance. Remember to talk about the concept of "turning around."*

4. *This story doesn't tell us in so many words that Zacchaeus had repented, but his actions tell their own tale. Encourage discussion of what repentance looks like.*

5. *Answers will vary. Talk about the dangers of gossip and of feeling superior to others.*

6. *This is a very important question. Many times, people have run into trouble with confession by including people who could not handle the burden. Talk about the importance of confessing to someone who is mature enough to help you, who is not of the opposite gender, who is not involved in the problem, and who is not going to gossip. Other points will probably come up as well.*

7. *Confession is powerful in breaking the bond of shame, and allowing us to seek help and to be set free. Because confession is for forgiveness and freedom, if someone confesses sin to you, your goal should be to actively seek this person's restoration. Answers will vary as you discuss the "how" of this question.*

8. *Emphasize the goal of restoration, not of finding out everyone's dirty little secrets, or starting a blackmail ring, or keeping everyone "humble" (or humiliated).*

Chapter 5: God Is Merciful

Focus: *It would be easy to view God's judgments as harsh or unfair, because after all, who enjoys punishment? But let's look beyond our initial rejection and consider a deeper question of who God really is, and why He gives us the limits that we find so hard to take.*

1. We often think of discipline only in terms of punishment, but the word actually indicates "training." While training may need to include punishment, or chastening, this is not the primary focus. Discipline includes instruction, rebuke, and guidance. Consider the investment of time and concern that must be included to train someone in a skill or discipline such as music, athletics, art, etc.

2. We have to realize that we don't always know what is going to be best for us. Encourage people to share experiences they have had that seemed negative, but that turned into something beneficial.

3. Answers will vary.

4. Chastening can be good discipline; giving us a strong incentive to stick to what is right. However, if we do not accept the discipline, then we can turn to rebellion, bitterness, self-pity, or anger.

5. If you run out into oncoming traffic, and you get hit, it wasn't because the driver of the car was punishing you for disobedience. You got hit because you got in front of a fast-moving vehicle. Repenting of your actions will keep you from doing it again, but it can't get you out of the hospital.

6. Don't get sidetracked on to a discussion of spanking here. Think about discipline in the broader sense of training. Parents have the God-given responsibility to train their children to follow God and to be responsible members of society. If parents do not train their children, they are cheating their children out of valuable life skills.

7. God's mercy is grand beyond our comprehension; it has provided life, light, and salvation.

8. The mercy of God is not just "feel good" fluff. God is righteous and holy, without sin or shadow. When He gives mercy it isn't because He doesn't know or care what has really been going on, but because He loves us and wants us to have the opportunity to be right. God judges all things, and He judges correctly. He knows all the facts, and all the answers.

Chapter 6: Forgive Me!

Focus: In order to receive forgiveness, we have to want it. The father of the wayward boy had forgiveness and restoration waiting, but it could not be given until the son returned.

1. We know that it is our responsibility to forgive those who wrong us (see **Matthew 5:43–48 and 6:9–15**), even if they are not sorry. We must do this order to prevent bitterness from growing in our lives and ruining us. By forgiving those who wrong us, we are deciding to not hold that person's sins against them, and to leave them entirely in God's hands. A forgiving spirit decides to harbor love instead of bitterness. In this sense, the forgiveness is for the benefit of the victim, not the sinner.

2. Restoration cannot occur without repentance. Restoration is the return to the way things should be. When you are going the wrong way, you cannot return without changing your direction. In the same way, a sinner must change direction (repent) in order to return (be restored).

3. *There is a reason that it is so hard to forgive someone who is not repentant. We have a very difficult time with this because this kind of forgiveness is only halfway. It helps us, as the victims of the abuse, but it doesn't "fix" anything about the problem. When we choose to forgive someone who is not repentant, we are not saying, "Oh, it doesn't matter." Forgiveness does not mean saying that there was nothing wrong with what happened. It means that we are choosing to turn the judgment over to God, and let Him take care of it. We are choosing to leave room in our hearts for love and compassion, not for bitterness or hatred.*

4. *Repenting and asking forgiveness from someone who had no mercy would do you no good. But God, like the father of the wayward son, is full of mercy and forgiveness. He is willing to restore us to abundant life now, and to the promise of life eternal.*

5. *In order to leave our sins, we have to be aware of what they are. Confession helps us to be specific. Saying, "Forgive me for anything bad I might have done," does not require us to actually admit anything. But in order to get rid of our sins, we have to look at them. Saying out loud, "I did this, I repent, and I reject this behavior" is very important in helping us to change.*

6. 7. *and* 8. *To come up with answers to these questions, compare the different reactions to realizing sin and the need for salvation. How are they the same? How are they different? How do they compare to the experiences of the members of this group? Encourage group members to explore the question of "the bottom line" and to back up their answers with the Bible.*

Chapter 7: God Seeks Sinners

> **Focus:** *God is not only willing to forgive and restore sinners, He actively seeks the unworthy to bring them back to His family. He goes out looking for the lost, just like Mr. Peggotty went looking for little Emily.*

1. It would be helpful for the leader to read these passages ahead of time and make a list of the things she sees. Encourage the group members to come up with their own lists, and use your list to keep things going if people get stuck.

2. See question 1.

3. Read **Ephesians 2:11–22**.

4. Encourage participants to think this out together.

5. See **Colossians 1:21–22**.

6. Answers will vary.

7. Whether or not Saul was aware that this was Jesus, his response is interesting.

8. Remember that Saul was present at the stoning of Stephen. Read **Acts 7**, and think about the effect Stephen's message might have had on Paul.

9. Tie this in with the question from last week about what repentance looks like.

Chapter 8: For a Worthless Sinner?

Focus: *God wanted us to be in right relationship with Him so much that He was willing to pay the price. No one pays a high price for something that he or she considers worthless. He saved us because He could see our potential, and thought we were worth rescuing.*

1. Without Christ, we are without strength to overcome our sin.

2. Answers will vary.

3. Someone who is deserving probably also doesn't need the sacrifice. It is so important to realize that Jesus did not pay the price because He owed it to us, but because He loves us.

4. An author creates; Jesus is the One who created a way for us to come to Him. Read **2 Timothy 1:12** and **Philippians 2:13** in thinking about Jesus as the finisher of our faith.

5. Discuss what it means for Jesus to consider it a joy to save us.

6. Encourage everyone to stop and imagine the scene in Gethsemane.

7. *Read also 1 John 1:1–4; John 20:26–29.*

8. *Answers will vary.*

Chapter 9: God's Forgiveness Is Complete: He Brings Restoration

Focus: *Not only does God cleanse us and make us like new, He also brings us home, restored to our original owner. God's forgiveness is complete.*

1. *Use a dictionary to help you with precise definitions of these words. Encourage group members to come up with examples of the difference between power and authority. For instance, a policeman has both the authority (given by the state or city) to enforce the law, but he also has the power (a gun and a fast car) to force obedience if need be.*

2. *Suppose you go on a sugar binge, break into a convenience store, and steal $160.00 worth of candy. As you step out of the store with your loot, a passing county sheriff sees you, and picks you up. As he puts you into his car for the ride to the station, a passerby comes up to you and says warmly, "Don't worry, honey, I forgive you!" Would this do you any good?*

3. *See also Acts 2:22–36; 1 Corinthians 15:1–19.*

4. *Use a dictionary to define the word remission. Tie this question in with the previous discussion of repentance and restoration.*

5. *See also* **1 Thessalonians 1:10; Romans 5:1.**

6. *The word* reconcile *can be used in the realm of friendships or other relationships, meaning to bring disagreeing parties back into a state of harmony or agreement. It can also be used in reference to financial matters, such as reconciling your checkbook. Again, it means "to bring into agreement" (in this case, bringing your checkbook into agreement with your bank statement).*

7. *Read* **Genesis 3:8–9; 22–24** *ahead of time and make a list of the clues you find. Use this list to help the discussion, but encourage participants to do their own searching.*

8. *Also read* **Matthew 19:27–30; Romans 8:15–19; Revelation 21:7.**

Chapter 10: Embracing Forgiveness

Focus: *God's forgiveness makes all things new. Don't dwell on past failures. Instead, take up the new life He offers and build again.*

1. *All who have believed on the Lord Jesus are promised eternal life (see* **John 3:16; Acts 16:30–31**). *We also look forward to a time when we will understand all that troubles us, and when all will be made right (* **1 Corinthians 13:9–13**).

2. *Answers will vary.*

3. *If we continue to dwell on all our past wrongs, we can cripple ourselves with guilt and fear. By focusing on what is bad, our hearts and thoughts are darkened, and we find it difficult to move on. While we may not be able to actually forget our sins, we can choose not to dwell on them, or continue to act in that mode. At the same time, it is an important safeguard to be aware of what our own weaknesses are.*

4. *Restoration means a return to our original design and purpose, including living righteously and joyously. Encourage group members to think of examples of what it means to be restored in soul.*

5. *Tie this in with your other discussions on the need for repentance to complete the transaction of forgiveness.*

6. *It is important for us to realize that feeling that we are "too bad" to be forgiven is just as big a mistake as feeling "too good" to need it. Jesus tells us over and over that He came to save sinners because we are the ones who need it. Peter was one of Jesus' closest friends, and he completely failed the Lord in His hour of deepest grief and need. He was "too bad," and yet the Lord loved him and wanted him.*

7. *Read the first four chapters of the book of Acts to get a picture of who Peter turned out to be. Peter was given the opportunity to go back to the very place where he had failed, and have another chance to boldly take his stand as "one of those followers of Jesus."*

8. *Answers will vary.*

Chapter 11: The Clean Slate

Focus: From God, forgiveness and cleansing
go hand in hand.

---

1. Encourage the group to think of other metaphors that indicate immeasurable distance. Because our debt has been paid, God can erase the "balance due" side of our ledger, and give us a clean start. Read the rest of **Psalm 103** as you prepare for this lesson.

2. If God really removes our transgressions from us, giving us a clean start, then whatever was in our background ceases to matter. God uses hearts that are yielded to Him, now, today. A perfect past or an imperfect past can, either one, be used greatly by God if we let Him. A good example of this is the contrast between Paul and Timothy. Timothy was raised by two godly women, and even as a young man showed a spiritual maturity and godly character that was an example and encouragement to the rest of the church. Paul had spent his time persecuting and murdering God's people, yet when he repented, he was mightily used of God to spread the gospel and build up the church.

3. Encourage group members to talk about how an ideal father responds to his children. God is not only our loving Father, but our Creator. He knows exactly what we are made of, and what we are made for.

4. At the time of Jesus' ministry on earth, it was the job of a courteous host to offer a foot bath to his guests. Roads were dry, dusty, and rough, and a traveler on foot would have tired, dirty feet. To provide your guest with the soothing comfort of clean feet

was appropriate hospitality, just as a comfortable chair and a glass of ice water are today. Washing someone's feet was also an act of humble service (see **John 13:3–16**).

5. We think of the Pharisees as the "bad guys" of the New Testament, because Jesus rebuked their hypocrisy so severely, and because they ended up leading the opposition to the early church. It is important for us to realize, however, that the Pharisees were the "good guys" originally, the ones who were determined to return to the Lord and follow His law, and to never again be guilty of turning away from God to idols. Simon, the Pharisee, was probably very sincerely religious, and he had worked hard to keep God's law all his life. In contrast, the woman was probably an adulteress, or maybe even a prostitute. She had a very bad reputation, but perhaps it was her evil situation that gave her such a clear view of who Jesus was and how much she needed Him. Someone in Simon's position could much more easily be lulled into feeling that he was performing adequately.

6. Answers will vary.

7. Humans have a fear of being underwater for too long. No matter how dense or ignorant we are, humans instinctively know that breathing water is bad for us. Baptism is a graphic, physical picture of the reality of our spiritual rebirth; something that any human could grasp the significance of. We know that going underwater for too long spells death for air-breathing creatures; coming back up again is a clear picture of being brought back to life.

8. Read **1 Corinthians 15:1–19** again.

9. Answers will vary.

Chapter 12: Forgive As You Have Been Forgiven

Focus: *God's kindness to us in His knowledge of our weakness is a precious thing. In the same way we must extend kindness to our fellow humans when they err. We know their weaknesses all too well, for they are the same as our own.*

1. *Keep the answers to these questions brief, just as a preliminary to the rest of the discussion.*

2. *and 3. Read* **Ephesians 4:31–5:2** *and* **Colossians 3:12–14** *as you prepare for this lesson; use a dictionary to help you with your lists and definitions, so that you can facilitate the discussion during the study. Encourage participants to come up with examples of these behaviors.*

4. *God wants us to obey him, but not just for his sake. When we obey him, not only do we represent God in a positive way to those around us, but we enrich our own lives.*

5. *Encourage group members to come up with examples of what it might look like to "put on love" or "walk in love." The image of "putting on love" like a coat or a hat is an interesting thought to explore. Talk about the concept of love as a choice more than as just a feeling.*

6. *It is important to recognize that forgiveness does not mean saying what happened didn't matter. When someone has been*

hurt, it is vital for that person to understand that God does not consider it "okay" that it happened. Forgiveness is not denial; it is releasing the problem to God's justice and mercy.

7. *Read **Matthew 18:21–35**. God forgives us again and again. We, too, are to forgive unconditionally.*

8. *No. The master was merciful. The servant, too, should have shown mercy—forgiveness—to his debtors.*

THE COMPLETE WOMEN OF FAITH®
STUDY GUIDE SERIES

OVERCOMING FEAR

UNDERSTANDING PURPOSE

RECEIVING GOD'S GOODNESS

RECEIVING GOD'S LOVE

CONTAGIOUS JOY

A LIFE OF WORSHIP

DISCOVERING GOD'S WILL FOR YOUR LIFE

CULTIVATING CONTENTMENT

EXPERIENCING SPIRITUAL INTIMACY

GIVING GOD YOUR ALL

LIVING ABOVE WORRY AND STRESS

AMAZING FREEDOM

MANAGING YOUR MOODS

LIVING IN JESUS

ENCOURAGING ONE ANOTHER

KNOWING GOD'S WORD

LIVING A LIFE OF BALANCE

ADVENTUROUS PRAYER

To find these and other inspirational products visit your local Christian retailer.

WOMEN OF FAITH

THOMAS NELSON
Since 1798